Tír na nÓg

Justin Wiggins

impspired@gmail.com

ISBN: 978-1-914130-54-0

OTHER TITLES BY IMPSPIRED

Daddy –
by Jon Koker

The Blue Hour -
By Annie 'Lisa' Harpel

Beautiful Boy –
By Joseph Mykut

Marty & Irene
By Justin Wiggins

Old Wood Shop –
By Charlie Brice & Jim Hutt

Immersed in Blue –
By Margaret Royall

Island –
By Clair Chilvers

Skinless in the Cereal Aisle –
By Scott Ferry

I dedicate this book to my dear friends David Jack and Jessica Jack along with Colin Duriez and Cindy Zudys.

Contents

Foreword

By Ger White

From the mountains of North Carolina Justin Wiggins takes us on a literary journey through Scotland, Ireland, England, and America. A journey of despair, depression, hope, adventure, and yearning. A journey shared by many other great writers. He openly shares with us his emotions of physically walking in the footsteps of great writing heroes, his respect, his joy, and how these heroes further his urge to continue writing.

We get education into C.S. Lewis's great yearnings from crisis to a knowledge of the true love of Christ, which I learned from the author, is ultimately the only love. The author explores works of over 20 writers (from Ireland, Scotland, England, America) – with quoted passages and examples – showing life's meaning and hope.

Tír na nÓg, Wiggins tells us, evokes the sehnsucht mystical joy, experienced by C.S. Lewis and written about in his books, as well as carrying the traditional Irish meaning of Land of the Forever Young.

This was an educational read for me. Wiggins highlights many writer's worldview perspectives on Joy and on being in the Here and Now. He covers writers from ancient Ireland through to modern writings, covering, C.S. Lewis, Seamus Heaney, John

O'Donohue, James Joyce, Oscar Wilde, William Butler Yeats, Neil Gaiman, the Brontë sisters, Charles Dickens, John Keats, Jane Austen, J.R.R. Tolkien, William Shakespeare, Dorothy Sayers, Frederick Buechner, John Steinbeck, Jon Foreman, George MacDonald, and others, all on journeys of hope and how they dealt with despair, loneliness, and found joy, healing, and hope.

This is a rich educational book showing a deep respect of writers, musicians, and poets, and all forms of Art, and the value of artists in society.

I could sum up this book by saying that for me it asked the question "What sparks joy?" and answered the question in a myriad of ways with many examples from great writers, and even more beautifully in the author's own honest voice.

Thanks Justin – I look forward to many more books in your name.

Introduction

By Justin Wiggins

The most beautiful place that I have seen on this earth is The Cliffs of Moher in Ireland. The place is a popular tourist spot, but is still certainly worth seeing, and I am thankful that my green converse shoes made their way to the land of the Tuatha dé Danann-it was an answer to prayer. For years I yearned to see the country where great writers like William Butler Yeats, Seamus Heaney, Oscar Wilde, John O' Donohue, and my favorite writer, C. S. Lewis, was born. I got a lot of creative inspiration for writing in Ireland, was shown great hospitality by some Irish friends, met some very friendly locals, enjoyed good food, good books, coffee, tea, soda bread, and some Jameson, and Guinness of course. While I was at the glorious Cliffs of Moher, I thought about how out of death comes life - I was close to death years ago, and yet, out of that great crisis, came great joy, healing, community, a renewed faith, and an epic trip to Scotland, England, and Ireland.

When I was in Ireland, I found myself filled with sehnsucht-years ago I did not know how to articulate this peculiar desire within myself to know who I was created to be, and why my life was significant, until I read C. S. Lewis. His life story of chasing this sweet great yearning led him to the same Christ whose love continues to make all things new today, and like

Emeth, who in The Last Battle comes to know whom he was always longing for when he finally meets Aslan in the true Narnia, so did I come to know the risen Christ, whose scarred hands healed my wounds, and gave my life meaning and hope.

Like Lewis, I had a complete worldview change through the influence of his writings, just as he did by reading the great Scotsman George MacDonald, and over the years my faith has been strengthened by the pain and joy of being alive on this planet and learning from different worldview perspectives other than my own. It is good to be alive, and I look forward to many more epic adventures!

This book, which expresses my love for the mountains of North Carolina, different parts of America, Ireland, Scotland, and England, was birthed by a much needed holiday I took in September and October of 2021, which changed my life.

I had been to England once before, but I had not yet had the opportunity to experience the beauty and culture of Ireland and Scotland. That trip was life changing, and I got to spend my birthday in Dublin.

This book that you are reading was inspired by that amazing trip. I chose the title Tír na nÓg because the ancient myth about the eternal land of beauty and youth evokes that mystical joy C. S. Lewis wrote about in many of his books. Lewis was told about this mystical place as a young lad growing up in Belfast, Northern Ireland by his nurse. The myth, as well as the landscape of Ireland, roused that mystical joy which led him from the paradigm of a staunch atheistic empirical rationalism to a spiritual view of the world which gave his life great meaning and hope. That mystical joy, which I believe to be a universal human longing that transcends time and culture, was very important in my own life in coming to embrace faith in Christ from Agnosticism years ago.

The writers from each different country, in their own worldview perspective, convey that same joy to me, and that joy is also latent in the poems and short stories in this book - the unifying factor is what the Tír na nÓg myth evokes about the sweet joy experienced in the present by millions around the world.

For myself, that mystical joy reminds me of the importance of the here and now in the context of eternity, and as an artist, I try and write honest and hopeful things for people of all worldviews- I like sharing that joy. For different poets, musicians, writers, painters, and artists, that joy is something universal, regardless of the individual's life philosophy. Joy is such a precious gift! A couple has a handfasting wedding ceremony in the Highlands of Scotland, an older lady tells a young lad working in a bookshop about how she beat cancer, a writer gets to hold a copy of her book for the first time in her life and do a book signing where a community come out to support her; a band gets their first record deal, a young man graduates with his M.A. in counseling and psychology and is able to help people find healing and hope; a couple that has been married for 50 years celebrate their golden wedding anniversary in the mountains of North Carolina. All of these are instances of people experiencing the gift of joy in this very brief life that we have.

I hope that this book brings you encouragement, inspiration, and joy. Thanks for reading! Slainte!

Acknowledgements

I want to say thanks to Steve Cawte of Impspired for publishing *Marty & Irene,* and for publishing *Tír na nÓg*, to the writer friends that have endorsed this book, and to everyone who encouraged me to finish it. Writing it helped me combat trauma, helped me find joy and healing, reminded me of why I do what I do, and brought back rich memories I made in England, Scotland, and Ireland. Cheers!

Ode to Books, Ode to Oxford & North Carolina were previously published in *Poetica 1 and Poetica 2 Inner Circle Writer's Group Poetry Anthology* by Grant Hudson of Clarendon House Publications and used with permission.

The two essays on J. R. R. Tolkien and George MacDonald were originally published in *Surprised by Myth, Essays On The Inklings and Their Friends* that I co-wrote with Grant Hudson of Clarendon House Publications.

Mystical Mountains, Healing Celtic Song, and *Tír na nÓg,* were previously published in paperback and kindle anthologies by Steven Lester Carr of Sweetycat Press, and are used with permission.

The Writer story, originally published in *Journeys Writer's Journey Blog,* is used with permission by Elaine Marie Carnegie-Padgett

Ireland

C. S. Lewis: Narnia, Ireland & Till We Have Faces

Although my favorite writer, C. S. Lewis, lived most of his life in England, he was Northern Irish born and bred, and always had a great affection for the island he was born on. No doubt certain parts of Oxfordshire and Cambridge in England inspired his wonderful Narnia books, but it was the landscape of Northern, Ireland that fired his Celtic imagination when he was subconsciously creating the world that Aslan sings into being that millions around the world have experienced on this side of the wardrobe. I had a very powerful spiritual experience when reading that particular part in *The Magician's Nephew* for the first time, and I was never the same person again - it was a revelation to me of why myth and storytelling is so important to humanity.

When I first started seriously reading Lewis, studying his works, and reading biographies on him, I was very intrigued to find out exactly what inspired him to write *The Chronicles of Narnia.* His essays, letters, poetry, literary criticism, theological and philosophical works, and other fiction are all very important and worth reading, but his Narnia books have been his most popular, and there are numerous reasons why. One reason why is that Lewis wrote about universal themes of peril, danger, adventure, joy, love, friendship, and redemption in the form of fairy tales.

Writers like Phillip Pullman have critiqued the books, as well as many others, but many scholars such as Colin Duriez, Don King, Malcolm Guite, modern writers like Neil Gaiman and Patti Callahan Henry, and millions of people around the world have found great inspiration, enchantment, and hope from these amazing books - quite incredible that all of this began with a picture Lewis had in his mind of a faun with an umbrella walking in a snowy wood with a young girl. The characters Mr. Tumnus and Lucy Pevensie are forever immortalized. It was very special getting to see the lamppost at Campbell College in Belfast which gave Lewis that very special visual image that sowed the seed for the book years later in his life.

One reason I am so fond of the Narnia series, is that the books actually helped me to learn how to read and write, and ever since then, I have had a great affection for them. Before reading them, I had a slight stuttering problem, was quite shy, and had the attention span of a goldfish! That changed dramatically after I read each of those powerful books. Usually, people have them read to them when they are children by their parents or grandparents, but for me I discovered them late in life, but, as Providence would have it, I read them at just the right time!

One of the most exciting experiences of being in

Ireland, is that I got to see, in person, the city of Belfast where Lewis was born, and the landscape which inspired his Narnia mythology. My Irish writer friend Judith Millar was kind enough to show me the Lewis places in Belfast, for which I am thankful. I was sad to see that the first home Lewis was born in was destroyed but delighted to see that the Little Lea home where he grew up in is still intact, even though it is not owned by the C. S. Lewis Company or The C. S. Lewis Foundation. One of the best parts of that golden September day in Belfast with my friend Judith was getting to visit The Lamppost Café. The place was charming, cozy, and filled with books, visual art inspired by beloved characters of Narnia, and to my amusement, I even saw an icon of St. C. S. Lewis, which Jack probably would have loathed. To me, the Irishman is a Saint.

As I am writing this, I look at my Celtic cross I am wearing, which is a very important icon to me. I purchased the talisman at the beautiful Dunluce Castle in Ireland. I can still remember trembling with excitement walking around Dunluce Castle, which is Cair Paravel. The high winds, the vast expanse of sea, the bright vivid shades of green, and the ruins of that place all certainly evoked the numinous and felt like Narnia - I was in what the Celts referred to as a thin place. When I was there, I imagined to myself what it was like for the young Lewis to go on adventures there when he would go with his Mother Flora, and his brother Warnie. Getting to visit Dunluce Castle was the closest that I will get to Narnia on this side of Heaven. As much I loved seeing Lewis's home in England where he wrote some of the Narnia books, the pilgrimage I took to Ireland made me feel I had actually crossed over into Narnia, and someday I look forward to thanking the Irishman in Aslan's country - when I take the last journey from the shadowlands to the true Narnia, where he is now with his beloved wife Joy Davidman, rejoicing and laughing.

It is very moving to me that Joy Davidman, who would eventually become Lewis's wife, was taken on a trip to Ireland with Jack Lewis after they were married. The American Jewish writer and poet inspired Lewis to finish his book *Till We Have Faces* which was published in 1956, and was dedicated to his wife. This work of fiction by Lewis is very different from *The Chronicles of Narnia, The Great Divorce, The Screwtape Letters*, and *The Space Trilogy,* and Lewis thought it was his best work he ever wrote. The story is set in a pre-Christian period, comes from the perspective of the female heroine Orual, and is Lewis' version of the ancient Greek myth of Cupid and Psyche. The myth is very well written, engaging, challenging, and is full of many Christian themes. The strongest theme, in my opinion, is the theme of how divine love needs to redeem human love. In the story Orual is jealous and obsessive over her beautiful sister Psyche. She feels robbed because the god of the mountain takes her away, and she comes to believe that the gods are capricious, that she should have possession of her sister. Orual is also possessive over the warrior Bardia, and in the end is the cause of his death because of how much he helped her physical with training and journeying to find Psyche. Throughout the book Orual goes through these series of experiences where she finally comes to be confronted with how her human love erred, and is in need of redemption. Her complaint against all of the gods ends up being the answer that she was looking for all along, and she comes to finally have a face. Orual finally comes to a place of surrender, repentance, and understanding in the very end of the book. It takes going through very painful experiences to get to this point, but she finally does. This theme of human love needing to be redeemed by divine love that C.S.Lewis writes so poignantly about in this mythical story is an important theme on one's own odyssey of faith. We all struggle with being possessive over someone, whether it be a family member, friend, or lover. It is in our nature. We worry, we don't want to lose something we love, and therefore an innocent love can actually become an idol.

I have experienced this personally, and in the end, it hurt like hell, and there were some very traumatic experiences I went through which raised huge questions, but in the end, the experience gave me understanding. It helped me to understand that romantic love could not fully satisfy the longing and yearning in my heart for The Creator.

This has still been a great struggle for me and is something I know other individuals deal with in the context of their own experience. This theme of human love needing to be redeemed by divine love is one of the main themes of C. S. Lewis' incredible book *The Four Loves* which was first published in 1960. In this book, which was edited some by Lewis' wife Joy Davidman, explores the four Greek loves that make up our human existence. The very last chapter is about Agape love, which is The Creator's love for humanity. Lewis very brilliantly (as always) ends the book by saying that friendship, affection, and romantic love are good in themselves, but not enough. They can easily become an idol. This is something every human being experiences at some point. It is often painful, difficult, and raises huge questions. Lewis argues that divine love is needed to redeem these human loves. When these loves are centered in divine love, then they are enjoyed for what they were meant to be.

I have known this by personal experience. I relate to this great theme in Lewis' *Till We Have Faces,* and *The Four Loves,* because since I am a romantic, I have struggled greatly with putting romantic relationships before The Creator. It took going through some very painful things to come to a place of surrender, where I finally "found my face." When one gets to this point, then true understanding comes. It is an understanding about how much of a gift these loves are from The Creator, and that His Agape love is what we need the most. When everything is centered around the Agape Love of Christ, then everything is in harmony, and we can experience the richness of family love, friendship, romantic love, and divine love as it was meant to be. These incredible gifts give one a glimpse of what the marriage of heaven and earth will be like.

In 2022, I found myself feeling quite stuck, depressed, and lonely- sometimes many things can hit you all at once, and I needed to be reminded of why I believe what I believe, why I do what I do, and all the good sacramental things that make this life worth living, so I picked up my favorite book by my favorite writer, C. S. Lewis- *Surprised By Joy*. Re-reading that amazing and fascinating book by the great Irish writer, helped pull me out of a jaded cynicism, and it made me feel alive again. Lewis writing poignantly about his rich childhood in Northern Ireland, the sad loss of his Mother, hellish experiences in WWI, embracing of atheism, his friendships at Oxford, intense experience of the 'Sehnsucht' mystical joy roused by Celtic and Norse mythology, George MacDonald's writings, landscape, music, and art, and his journey to embracing faith in Christ from atheism, is such a fascinating story. My favorite part in the book is when

Lewis writes about his mystical experience of joy when reading the great Scottish writer MacDonald's book *Phantastes,* which is a very strange and beautiful fantasy book, and another favorite part is when Lewis states that his experiences as a literary scholar convinced him that the first century Gospels were historical, and the story of Jesus of Nazareth's Incarnation, Death, and Resurrection is "the true myth."

The book reminded me of my own experiences of Sehnsucht- the music of Jon Foreman, Frederic Chopin, Celtic and Nordic music, the mountain landscape of my native state North Carolina, the landscape of England, Ireland, and Scotland, the season of Autumn, memories made in coffee shops, bookstores, and pubs; the poetry of John Keats, Wendell Berry, the writings of J. R. R. Tolkien, Neil Gaiman, Madeleine L'Engle, George MacDonald, and Lewis of course, and rich memories. God bless the Irishman who inspired me to write this book Tír na nÓg.

Seamus Heaney: A Poet of the Irish & Everyone

I first read Seamus Heaney's translation of *Beowulf* when I was attending East Carolina University - before I went through a dark night of the soul and had a nervous breakdown. I had never heard of the Irish poet before, and his translation of that great epic poem helped me understand it, and thus I was overwhelmed by Northernness, as C.S. Lewis was. Years later, when I became stable, I purchased a wonderful book of his poems simply called *100 Poems* during the Winter of 2020. That book reminded me of how far I have come, and Heaney quickly became one of my favorite writers from Ireland. Reading poems of his like *Digging* and *The Cure At Troy* made me aware of Heaney's love for the earth, the Irish landscape, and the great joy he experienced in teaching poetry, in writing, and also getting his hands dirty by helping his father on the farm while growing up. When I was visiting some friends in Cullybackey Northern, Ireland, I didn't realize that Seamus Heaney was buried near where we were staying, and the kind Irish couple that was hosting me was kind enough to drive me to his grave.

I really loved the architecture of the beautiful St. Mary's Catholic Church where Heaney is buried, and while I was at his grave, I took a moment to express my gratitude with a prayer, a smile on my face, and a tip of my hat to Heaney's Celtic ancestors for blessing the world with such a gifted poet.

A few days later, I had the opportunity to experience the Seamus Heaney HomePlace in Bellaghy, Ireland. The place which was once a police station is quite impressive, and one could spend all day there. I was overwhelmed, even with the very loud students there that day I smiled at as I thought about what it was like being a teenager. I loved the library, the café, the little bookshop, and enjoyed talking with two friendly Irish ladies and a jovial Scotsman that worked there - he expressed his distaste for midges.

While I was walking around the exhibit, listening to audios of Heaney himself reading his poems, I found myself seeing a life well lived to the fullest, and it gave me an even greater desire to make the most of my brief life in the here and now. Seamus Heaney was a very gifted academic, poet, and is well respected by many actors, artists, musicians, and a poet of the people. I really appreciate it when an artist sees themselves just like everyone else and strives to live out the virtue of humility.

I walked out of that the Seamus Heaney Homeplace with a greater love for poetry, life, and I purchased a good writers pen that I have shockingly not lost yet, and I hope that it stays that way.

John O' Donohue: Anam Cara

In our postmodern world it can be quite difficult to find genuine people who know how to communicate, are truly there for you, and that speak your language - kindred spirits. There are many distractions in our technological age, but, fortunately, as in every era, there do exist those people one finds who are kindred spirits. With these people you can connect with beyond a mere superficial level, and if it is simply a few friends or many, it is a cause for rejoicing when the connection is made. Since the beginning, our human tribe has delighted in finding those people who get us. Perhaps no other writer has written so poignantly about kindred spirits than Irish poet, scholar, and philosopher, John O'Donohue.

His wonderful book, *Anam Cara: A Book of Celtic Wisdom,* made me feel less alone when I first read it, and made me aware of what a gift it is to have genuine people in your life in a shallow world of facades, superficiality, and hollow consumerism. It is quite difficult to serve The Creator and not mammon in our culture, but by grace, it can be done, thank God! *Anam Cara* was the first book that I read by the great Irish poet, and after that I read anything by him that I could get my hands on. I really like the way O' Donohue references many poets, philosophers, and thinkers from different religious and spiritual traditions, and his emphasis on mythology, imagination, community, Celtic spirituality, and finding rhythms in daily life which brings joy, and gives one balance between their reason and emotions.

One great Anam Cara in my life is my friend Andrew Jackson. We have known each other for about ten years, and my third book, *Marty & Irene* was dedicated to him. No one on this planet can make me laugh like he can. Once I was feeling quite hopeless and felt trapped inside a hospital after attempting suicide; but what a great joy it was to see my friend Andrew Jackson walk through the door to my room! I was not expecting to see him that day, and that visit from him reminded me that my life is worth living. I remember how lonely, confused, and depressed I was years ago. I didn't have many friends, I didn't have much to look forward too, and I didn't know what I was going to do with my life.

Eventually, I embraced a worldview that gave my life meaning, and I began to find many kindred spirits - these amazing 'Anam Cara's' and found that I wasn't alone. One very special memory stands out when I was at a Oxfam charity shop in Dundee, Scotland with my Scottish friend David Jack, and as we were both perusing the shelves, I turned to look after he told me to come over and he handed me a copy of poetry by O'Donohue called *Conamara Blues.* It was one I had been yearning to read with great excitement, and there it was finally in my hands at a charity shop in bonny Scotland! I finished reading that book by the sea in Ireland. Thank goodness for Anam Cara's!

In 2008 many people around the world mourned the loss of the great Irish poet, philosopher, and scholar John O' Donohue. I wish I would have had the chance to meet him as I have had with many other writers, poets, musicians, artists, and philosophers that I admire. His books and teachings have helped so many people in our very polarized post-modern world experience a great sense of wonder and the divine in everyday life. He was a great Irishman that had a glimpse of Tír na nÓg in this life.

James Joyce

When I was in community college, I picked a copy of James Joyce's *A Portrait of The Artist As A Young Man* and tried to give it a read but wanted to throw the book against the wall when I got about 30 pages into it. Each page I turned in the dreadful book was a chore, and I hoped that maybe I could somehow become immersed in the narrative, but I couldn't bear his bizarre stream of consciousness any longer.

What eventually gave me an appreciation for him as an Irish writer worth reading, was his poignant story *The Dead.* I had to read it for a class assignment, and I was horrified- not again! How unprepared I was to come to actually appreciate the great Irish writer who is often criticized for an incomprehensible stream of consciousness which comes across as pretentious. *The Dead* was completely different from the first book I tried to read by him, and I found it to be an amazing piece of work.

The second time I re-read it, I purchased a copy of *Dubliners* from a Barnes and Noble where I used to work and read the book with great interest. Some of the stories in the book were sad, depressing, gritty, comical, but also fascinating, and moving, especially the last one, *The Dead,* and it was my second time reading it. Reading *The Dead,* was an important reminder to me of the brevity of life, what a gift it is to be alive, loved, and appreciated, and how utterly enchanting a quiet snowfall is.

I love these quotes below Joyce's brilliant and poignant story, "In one letter that he had written to her then he had said: Why is it that words like these seem to me so dull and cold? Is it because there is no word tender enough to be your name?"
"Yes, the newspapers were right: snow was general all over Ireland. It was falling on every part of the dark central plain, on the treeless hills, falling softly upon the Bog of Allen and farther westward, softly falling into the dark mutinous Shannon waves. It was falling, too, upon every part of the lonely churchyard on the hill where Michael Furey lay buried. It lay drifted on the crooked crosses and headstones, on the spears of the little gate, on the barren thorns. His soul swooned slowly as he heard the snow falling faintly through the universe and faintly falling, like the descent of their last end, upon all the living and the dead."(1) James Joyce

In the end it was a compulsory short story reading for a college course that gave me an appreciation for Joyce. Someday I may attempt to read *Finnegan's Wake or Ulysses,* but I am glad to have read *Dubliners,* which is a great tribute to the city Joyce was born in.

Oscar Wilde

When I was in the Charles De Gaulle airport in Paris, France I thought about the great playwright, poet, and Irish writer Oscar Wilde. It was in Paris where he died after being released from hard labor in prison-his once iconic reputation had been ruined by numerous affairs he had, which caused his downfall.

The first book I ever read by Oscar Wilde was a collection of his fairy tales called *The Happy Prince & Other Tales.* I had no idea about Wilde being part of the aesthete movement, what his worldview was, his great reputation as a playwright, his Irish roots, or the controversy that brought him to ruin in Victorian, England.

The most poignant of all the fairy tales was *The Selfish Giant.* I loved these lines from the story that convey the agape love of Christ through a fairy tale, "Who hath dared to wound thee?" cried the Giant; "tell me, that I may take my big sword and slay him." "Nay!" answered the child; "but these are the wounds of Love."

"Who art thou?" said the Giant, and a strange awe fell on him, and he knelt before the little child.

And the child smiled on the Giant, and said to him, "You let me play once in your garden, to-day you shall come with me to my garden, which is Paradise."

And when the children ran in that afternoon, they found the Giant lying dead under the tree, all covered with white blossoms." (2)

After reading that book of stories by Wilde, I got a copy of his *The Picture of Dorian Gray and Other Writings.* I found his play *The Importance of Being Earnest* funny and witty, as well as the film adaption starring the great actor Colin Firth, and Wilde's most iconic work, *The Picture of Dorian Gray* to be haunting, It is a poignant novel on the duality of human nature, complexity of sexuality, good and evil within the human heart, the search for meaning, and the emptiness, madness, and boredom that is behind a lavish hedonistic lifestyle. Whether you are religious or spiritual, non-religious, liberal, conservative, gay or straight, the amazing thing about a book like *The Picture of Dorian Gray,* is that it remains a timeless work of art because it resonates with the human heart. Each one of us has the potential to end up like Dorian Gray did, or we have the potential to choose goodness, beauty, and truth. I hope that Oscar Wilde found what he was looking for in the end.

William Butler Yeats

I became fascinated with the poetry of William Butler Yeats when I read C. S. Lewis's brilliant autobiography *Surprised By Joy.* I was intrigued by Lewis's encounter with Yeats' poetry when he was still an atheist and was coming close to believing in some kind of Spirit, Creator, or cosmic force. What impressed him about Yeats, is that not only was his poetry very good, but he was an Irishman that rejected the materialistic view of the world, and was a spiritual person that practiced esoteric mysticism, he believed in beings that one could communicate with, and that humans could encounter the divine in everyday life.

I first read a book of Yeats called *A Poet to His Beloved* and loved the melancholy, pain, and joy Yeats expressed in the different love poems, and from there I got my hands on a book all of his poems and some of his plays. Yeats' *The Lake Isle of Innisfree* gave me an intense love for Ireland, even though I had never been there, and his poems like *He Wishes for the Cloths of Heaven, Fergus and The Druid, When You Are Old, The Stolen Child,* and *A Prayer For My Daughter,* allowed me to understand and appreciate his amazing versatile work.

When I first saw the Irish sea from the plane as I was landing, and was walking the streets of Dublin, Yeats' *The Lake Isle of Innisfree* came to my mind, and

I was very glad to be in this beautiful country, founded by the Vikings. For his great poetry, Yeats was honored by his country by being given the Nobel Prize in literature in 1923, which is an amazing accomplishment that he certainly deserved. The amazing playwright, poet, mystic, is one of the greatest poets to ever come out of Ireland and is one I will always be quite fond of.

England

Neil Gaiman- Great Modern Mythmaker

I was working at a Books A Million at the time and was browsing around for something new to read. I wanted a good fantasy story that would be comforting, funny, have a good love story, involve some kind of quest or peril, have the Tolkienian happy ending, and make me feel like I was hearing a bard or skald in a mead hall, or around a bonfire with my people out under a starry luminous moonlit night. I just happened to come across a copy of Neil Gaiman's *Stardust.* The title and the cover of it intrigued me, and so I picked it up out of great interest, and that night I found myself being a great admirer of Gaiman.

I am glad that it was the first book I read by him, because I was a bit disappointed with *American Gods.* I really appreciated all the research he did on the different deities, and mythologies, but I just found the story, well, ok. It didn't really grip me like *Stardust* did. His *Coraline* reminded me of C. S. Lewis's *The Lion, the Witch, and The Wardrobe,* Brothers Grimm Fairy Tales, Ray Bradbury's *The October Country,* and Maurice Sendak's *Where The Wild Things Are.*

On my birthday, when I was browsing around Hodges Figgis bookshop in Dublin, Ireland back in September I saw a wonderful book by Neil Gaiman called *The View*

From The Cheap Seats, and I had to have it!
The amazing book is a compilation of book, music, film, and comic book reviews, talks and lectures on myth, imagination, reason, and the importance of art, libraries, and the courage and discipline it takes to be an artist.
My favorite essay from the book is "Three Authors. On Lewis, Tolkien, and Chesterton: The MythCon 35 Guest of Honor Speech." I appreciate the fact that Gaiman states it was C. S. Lewis, my favorite writer, who gave him the desire to become a writer at a very young age. I had the same experience. As much as I love Gaiman's fiction, this is certainly my favorite book by him, and one that I will return to again and again- a good writers bible.

Another good example of Neil Gaiman being an incredible mythmaker is his version of the Norse Mythology. Gaiman read the Poetic and Prose Eddas, and many other original sources when writing his own version of Norse Mythology. His book could have been a bore, but reading his *Norse Mythology* was like I was listening to a skald in a mead hall, telling me tales of creation, of Odin, Thor, Freya, Loki, Ragnar Lothbrok and his sons, the Sagas, and Ragnarök - the twilight of the gods when the world ends, and the gods die fighting against the Giants and Fenrir The Wolf, and how there is a new heaven and a new earth, and Balder, Odin's beloved son, comes back from the dead. The Nordic culture, religion, and myths are fascinating to me, and it was a common interest in these myths that allowed Lewis and Tolkien to become friends, and Tolkien helped Lewis understand how Christianity is the true myth. The dying and rising god story happened in first century Palestine through Jesus' Incarnation, death, and Resurrection.

On some very cold Winter nights I like to enjoy some mead and re-read Gaiman's wonderful book. I read a passage from it one night while hosting some friends for a pipe, pint, beer, food, coffee, and whisky night. It was grand. Thank you, Neil Gaiman, for writing *Norse Mythology,* and for your prodigious output of books. Skol!

The Bronte Sisters: Brief & Brilliant Lives

Among some of the great female writers that came from England, there is Emily, Anne, and Charlotte Brontë. I remember seeing a tribute center to the great female writers when I was in Ireland, but sadly, to my great regret, I didn't have time to see the place - one can't do everything when on holiday. The first book I read by the one of the Brontë sisters was Emily Brontë's *Wuthering Heights* when I was in community college. By then I was just starting to seriously to read, and I found the book to be not one that I could breeze through. After finishing, I gave it three out of five stars, and wasn't very moved by the narrative, but it gave me an appreciation for Emily Brontë, and the desire to read the other sisters.

It is quite sad that during the time they were growing up in Victorian England, they had to use pseudonyms when their wonderful and fascinating books were published. I, and many others around the world, are glad that Emily, Anne, and Charlotte were defiant of those cultural norms, and decided to write, while also being busy with doing domestic duties at their home in Haworth. Their great love for books is latent in their novels, and out of them all, *Jane Eyre* is by far my favorite. The book, which was originally published in 1847, is so well written, and was penned by a Yorkshire woman of Irish descent that was a genius. As I was reading it, I imagined to myself the kind of emotions Charlotte Brontë experienced while writing her book. I am sure she felt indescribable joy when she first got the news that she was a published writer! The story of the intelligent, pure, compassionate, independent, strong, and fairy sprite like Jane Eyre being an orphan, abused, bullied, psychologically manipulated by a fanatical school master, losing her friend Helen Burns, becoming a governess at Thornfield Hall; being horrified and heartbroken when she discovers that Mr. Edward Rochester has a wife who is insane that he was duped into marrying for money, and how she recovers, becomes a teacher, comes into an inheritance, connects with a long lost family she had no idea she had; and in the end ends up marrying Mr. Rochester after his insane wife sadly commits suicide, is a powerful story of loss, pain, how complex we are as people, hope, and the power of love.

I also noticed in the story the elements from myths and fairy tales that Charlotte Brontë incorporated, and I really loved her descriptions of nature, found her critique of cultural religious legalism amusing, and her writing to be poignant about the theological virtues of faith, hope, and love. This masterpiece of English literature was a joy to read and will be a book that I return to again and again. I hope one day, Lord willing, to read that book out in the Yorkshire Moors.

Charles Dickens

My first introduction to Charles Dickens was *Great Expectations*. The story about Pip, Miss Havisham, and his honest Uncle Joe, was a book that conveyed to me the value of an honest day's work, rustic country people, and the importance of family. I came to greatly appreciate Dickens long sentences, his ability to capture the different English dialects, and his creative way of coming up with creative names like 'Mr. Wopsle' or 'Mr. Pumblechook.' Dickens was a bit mad, but in a good way! It is amazing to me that the people in England would get in long lines to brave the cold for the next installment of a book from him.

My favorite of all Dickens work is by far, *A Christmas Carol.*
For many, Christmas is an ideal time for the giving of presents, kissing under the mistletoe, proposing, planning a wedding, wishing for a white snowy Christmas day, good food, laughs, having a much needed break from work, snowball fights, and watching films like *It's A Wonderful Life* and *Rudolph The Red Nosed Reindeer;* yet also for many, it is a time filled with grief, loss, stress, cynicism, and being haunted by the past, like Ebenezer Scrooge is in Charles Dickens classic work. One of the most heartbreaking parts in *A Christmas Carol* is when Scrooge, as a young man, chooses money over the

woman he was to marry. That is an appalling and evil thing. Fortunately for the woman, as shown by one of the spirits, finds a man worthy of her love; and fortunately for Scrooge, in the end, despite his sins in the past and worship of the god mammon, finds redemption and becomes a very jovial, benevolent, wise and loving individual.

This story, published in 1843, is a powerful universal work of art anyone can relate too, and has been one of the most popular books that has ever been written. It is a book I always look forward to reading during the Christmas season.

John Keats

The tragic and yet beautiful film *Brightstar* about the rapturous brief love between John Keats and Fanny Brawne gave me an amazing admiration for the romantic poet who died much too young. It's quite amazing how a film can give you a deeper understanding and greater appreciation for a writer, poet, musician, or artist that you admire. I love that about good films. Before I watched the film while working on my undergraduate degree in English Literature at Montreat College, I had read a few of Keats' poems such as *To Autumn, The Eve of St. Agnes, Ode on A Grecian Urn,* and *Ode to A Nightingale,* but after seeing that film, I got my hands on a beautiful paperback Vintage edition of Keats' poems and letters while I was at a Waterstones in Oxford, England. I still have that book, and each time I glance at it while taking a pause from my reading, it brings me right back to that very night the bookseller told me they had one copy, and I bolted upstairs to make sure it found its way into my hands.

John Keats was steeped in John Milton, Edmund Spenser, William Shakespeare, and mythology. His poetry is brilliant, captures the divine in the natural, and reminds me of the gift and brevity of life. It is very sad that he only lived until he was 25 and died in poverty; yet his legacy still lives on in his transcendent poetry. Many of my favorite writers praise his work, and I understand why. I often read and ponder this poignant poem of his about the brevity of life,

"When I have fears that I may cease to be
Before my pen has gleaned my teeming brain,
Before high-pilèd books, in charactery,
Hold like rich garners the full ripened grain;
When I behold, upon the night's starred face,
Huge cloudy symbols of a high romance,
And think that I may never live to trace
Their shadows with the magic hand of chance;
And when I feel, fair creature of an hour,
That I shall never look upon thee more,
Never have relish in the faery power
Of unreflecting love—then on the shore
Of the wide world I stand alone, and think
Till love and fame to nothingness do sink." (3)

Jane Austen

It is rather sad to me that Jane Austen wrote so many witty and moving books about love, but never married herself, which is ironic. Yet, her literary legacy lives on, and because of her inspiration, there are many Jane Austen societies around the world, many films and TV series have been done based off of her books, and they have delighted readers around the world with their charm, humor, and damn good love stories.

I started with *Pride and Prejudice* years ago after watching the long BBC version with the iconic Colin Firth playing Mr. Darcy. The funny and poignant story of Mr. Darcy and Elizabeth Bennett was a good introduction and won me over.

Of all her books I have read though, *Persuasion* is my favorite. It is a book about second chances, as two lost lovers find each other again after they thought all hope was lost after many years of suffering. I found it comical at how Austen poked fun at arranged marriages for money, and profoundly moving in how she told the story of Anne Elliot and Captain Wentworth. This is a very important book which gives the reader hope for second chances, whether it be at romantic love, being reconciled with a friend or family member, or another chance at pursuing a particular vocational path.

I have been given many second chances in my life that I feel as if I don't deserve it, but looking back, I am immensely thankful I was able to have that chance. In 2016 I moved away from Eastern, North Carolina to the mountains of North Carolina to a pursue my B.A. in English Literature with a focus on C. S. Lewis studies. When I first moved on the college's campus, I started to have flashbacks of traumatic events that happened to me when I was at a previous University years before. I eventually got to the point where I couldn't handle it, so like a fool, I decided to move back home, and I was absolutely horrified, and became severely depressed, but wonder of wonders - I was able to move back to the mountains of North Carolina to my utter joy.

I was given a second chance, and because of that second chance, I was able to have many rich life changing experiences I still marvel at. Thank you, Jane Austen, for writing such an amazing book about second chances.

J. R. R. Tolkien

I remember years ago browsing around this favorite used bookshop in Greenville, North Carolina, which is now sadly closed, and finding a paperback copy of Humphrey Carpenter's book called The Inklings which was first published in 1978. The book had been on my list to read for a while and finding it for quite cheap as a paperback was incredibly exciting.

By that point, I had read only a little of Lewis, Tolkien, Charles Williams, and MacDonald, so Carpenter's book was very enlightening on the dynamic friendship between the Inklings, differences in their personalities, views on literature and myth, different philosophical and theological views, and the bond of friendship and a mutual love for literature and story which kept the group meeting for many years.

Years later, I would have the opportunity to meet scholar and writer Colin Duriez, whose book The Oxford Inklings: Lewis, Tolkien, and Their Circle I have read many times. It was great meeting Colin in Montreat, North Carolina, at an Inklings retreat, and talking with him about Celtic Christianity, N. T. Wright, Charles Williams' view of co-inherence, his forthcoming book on Dorothy Sayers which is now out, and the shared admiration we both had of Lewis, Tolkien, and MacDonald's works. It was one of the best conversations of my life, and to my utter joy, years later, I would get to go on an Inklings tour with him and his wife Cindy Zudys on a fine March Day in Oxford. Going with them to Addison's walk, The Lamb and Flag pub, Magdalen College, Christ Church Meadow, and walking the streets of Oxford, was such a great delight. In conversation with Colin at The Lamb and Flag, I still vividly remember talking with him about the numinous evoked in Tolkien's work, and that gave me the desire to re-read The Lord of the Rings, which has become my favorite work of fiction.

It is amazing to me that although J. R. R. Tolkien sadly was an orphan, and lost many of his friends in the hell of World War I, he was still able to function, became an incredible Oxford professor, believed in a good and loving Creator, married his beloved Edith, who was also an orphan, and inspired his Luthien and Arwen characters in his mythology, and gave the world some great works of literature like *The Hobbit, The Silmarillion,* and his masterpiece *The Lord of The Rings.*

This man is such an inspiration to me, and his works have made me weep tears of joy; he inspires me to pursue my passion for writing, literature, and art, live out my faith, love people of different worldviews, love with passion, and strive to be gentle, kind, brave, honest, and jovial.

One of the most fascinating aspects from Tolkien's

mythology is the race of beings called hobbits. They represent very earthy and rustic people who love beer, coffee, pipe tobacco, the countryside, food, cheer, talk, tea, and sometimes, adventure. For generations, people around the world have been delighted with Bilbo Baggins adventure story of how he is taken out of his comfort zone and comes back a changed hobbit — this theme of exile and returning home certainly correlates to Tolkien's own life, and his mythology.

All of Tolkien's life was a journey to his true home in the presence of Christ, and he never abandoned that hope within him that he was taught by his mother; and though one can read *The Hobbit* and *The Lord of the Rings* simply for the joy of the stories in themselves (which is what Tolkien aimed to do) they are still filled with the faith which gave his life great joy and meaning.

Considering all the great loss and suffering Tolkien endured, I believe it was very brave of him to do what he did in his life with his writing, vocation as a philologist, the love he bore for his wife and family, and the faith in Christ which sustained him. It could have been very easy for Tolkien to reject what he was taught to be true at a young age, but, he defiantly affirmed his belief in a good and loving God, despite deep wounds which no doubt caused him much trauma and struggles with pessimism.

As a joke, my Scottish friend David Jack has called me 'Wiggins of Wig-End' which I take as a compliment, as many friends have also told me that I am very 'hobbit-like.' That compliment is an honor.

William Shakespeare - The Transforming Power of Love in Twelfth Night

In William Shakespeare's iconic whimsical comedy play *Twelfth Night,* the heroine, Viola who is disguised as Cesario, embodies how powerful redemptive love is, how it turns chaos into harmony, and how it turns tragedy into a happy ending. This redemptive love that she embodies has a powerful effect on every single individual in this play. Of all the female characters (there are many good one's) that I have read about in Shakespeare's plays, Viola is certainly my favorite because she does all that she can to find her brother when she finds herself in an unknown country, and she also ends up finding true love in the end through marriage after disguising herself as a man when she begins to work for Duke Orsino.

This masquerade of Viola's ends up bringing about a comical circumstance by Orsino coming to love Viola, and Viola coming to love Sebastian, the man who saved Viola's brothers life when he almost drowned.

I believe Shakespeare incorporates these elements of comedy and identity confusion in his plays to try and convey how powerful love is, how it can redeem confusion by bringing peace, and being a sacramental thing by bringing joy through marriage.

Although Shakespeare may or may have not been a Christian, he is writing within a Christian framework about what true love is. He was very familiar with The Bible, and ancient works of literature that were about love. I believe that through Viola's character he is saying what love is and what it is not. To him, it is nothing cheap, not a mere feeling, and not to be made small of. To him, it never gives up, makes people become more human, always hope's, brings joy and reflects the redemption of Christ.

One major and important example of Shakespeare's view of love is from the very beginning of the play- Viola does not give up when it comes to finding her brother. Although she comes to grips with the fact that he is possibly dead, yet she holds fast to hope. She is willing to disguise herself as a page, and to try and find out where her brother is. Through her perseverance and courage, Viola does find her brother, and beyond all hope, is reunited with him. She gives this moving speech when she reveals who she truly is,

> *"If nothing lets to make us happy both*
> *But this my masculine usurp' d attire,*
> *Do not embrace me till each circumstance*
> *Of place, time, fortune, do cohere and jump*
> *That I am Viola: which to confirm,*

> *I'll bring you to a captain in this town,*
> *Where lie my maiden weeds; by whose gentle help*
> *I was preserved to serve this noble count.*
> *All the occurrence of my fortune since*
> *Hath been between this lady and this lord." (4)*

Another really good example of how Viola embodies redemptive love is when she is wedded in the end to the duke that helped her find her brother. Because of this duke's power, she is able to travel freely without restrictions in the desperate search for her brother. In the end, the duke does not experience unrequited love, and to his hearts great desire, marries Viola.

Also in the end is another comical marriage of convenience when Belch marries Maria for getting her in trouble! Here again, we see something quite negative becoming something meaningful and beautiful because of the power of love. I really like the priest who gives this description of sacramental love in the play,

> *"A contract of eternal bond of love,*
> *Confirm'd by mutual joinder of your hands,*
> *Attested by the holy close of lips,*
> *Strengthen'd by interchangement of your rings;*
> *And all the ceremony of this compact*
> *Seal'd in my function, by my testimony:*
> *Since when, my watch hath told me, toward my*

grave
I have travell'd but two hours." (4)

As in all of Shakespeare's comedies, there is a happy ending in this play. Viola finds her long lost brother Sebastian after doing that all she can do to find him and thinking that he has died. Orsino and Viola have their heart's desire as they become one by forming a sacramental bond of devotion through marriage. Antonio is proved innocent as he explains to the duke how he saved Sebastian's life when he was going to die, is released from being a prisoner, and to Viola's utter joy and hope she is united with her brother Sebastian.

All the confusion and sorrow in this play is trumped by true love, which has the power to redeem, and bring meaning and joy to one's life.

Dorothy L. Sayers

One of my best memories of Oxford, England was walking the streets towards the witty and brilliant writer Dorothy Sayers home with my friend Colin Duriez, who is an amazing Tolkien, Lewis, and Inkling scholar, and his brilliant storyteller wife Cindy Zudys. It was a very wet, cold, and rainy October day in England, but still beautiful, and Colin and I got a picture of him holding a copy of my book *Surprised by Agape,* and I was holding a copy of his most recent biography on Dorothy Sayers called *Death, Dante, and Lord Peter Wimsey.* Being able to experience that was quite an honor and is a memory in Oxford I dearly cherish.

In 2022, I have finally started getting a greater appreciation for the mystery genre of literature. I recently started reading *Whose Body?* It is very witty, clever, and incredibly entertaining. I remember once talking with a lady at a used bookshop who had recommended the series to me, and she said, "Lord Peter Wimsey is cleverer than God!" I found the remark incredibly amusing, though I am not sure what Sayers would have thought of it. From Colin's biography, I was fascinated to learn that Sayers did advertising for my favorite beer, Guinness, worked for Blackwell's bookshop in Oxford for a period of time, and wrote some fascinating theological works, one of which is called *The Mind of the Maker*.

This book by Sayers, is a great theological manifesto on the joy people experience in their life co-creating with their Maker, whether they are gardening, writing a novel, a poem, or play, composing a song, painting a landscape, building a house, or whatever it might be. In the book Sayers puts a great emphasis on finding joy in the mundane and understanding that each person is on their own perilous and exciting odyssey in this life. Though Sayers was writing from a Christian worldview, perspective, anyone of whatever worldview can read and appreciate the work. The eccentric lady who loved her cigarettes, getting around on a motor scooter, was quite jovial, and translated Dante's masterpiece into English, sought to make Christianity exciting (as it began in the first century) to people who had a bad experience with cultural fundamentalism. Sayers did a damn good job of doing just that in her writings and life. She was an amazing woman.

America

Frederick Buechner

Losing someone you love to suicide leaves a profound wound in one's life. Could he or she have held on? Why did it happen? All these kinds of questions are raised when one experiences that great kind of loss. In dealing with the death of his father by suicide, the brilliant storyteller, man of hope, and theologian Frederick Buechner wrote many books in combating that grief. Of all the fiction and non-fiction books that he wrote, *Telling Secrets* is my favorite. I think it was very brave of Frederick Buechner to write about the deep wound his father's suicide left on him and his mother, and how he was able to find healing and hope in his life through the power of literature and art, and the agape love of Christ. He writes about faith in a way for people of all worldviews, in contrast to much of the cheesy, repetitive, and insincere propaganda nonsense out there which does not correlate to daily life.

Telling Secrets does not only deal with how he dealt with the loss of his father, but it also explores the horrific experience Buechner had of watching his daughter battle anorexia, and how he learned that as much as he wanted to, he could not save her, but she had to be willing to find healing and hope on her own, which she did, and it changed her life for the better. This book is good for anyone who has experienced great loss and painful seasons of grief, because the book is a great affirmation of hope. I read it at just the right time in my life when I needed too. I like the references Buechner's makes to J. R. R. Tolkien, George MacDonald, G.K. Chesterton, and C. S. Lewis, and his emphasis on the importance of stories.

In his book *The Sacred Journey*, which is the first book that I ever read by Buechner, he conveys how it was his love for story and narrative which helped him to embrace faith in Christ, and I am glad that happened to Buechner, since he writes for people who have been deeply wounded by organized religion, and people who grew up being exposed to a fundamentalist toxic theology. Though Buechner is a great theologian, his writings focus more on the reality of grace being a free unmerited gift, and the journey of faith, being a story told by The Great Storyteller- a paradox of human choices and the sovereign grace of Christ. I am thankful for the great storyteller and theologian.

Madeleine L'Engle

One of the amazing things to me about Madeleine L 'Engle's *A Wrinkle In Time,* is that the book was rejected numerous times by many publishers, which was very difficult for her, but L'Engle was persistent, and eventually her book was published in 1962 and won the Newberry Medal Award, which is quite an amazing accomplishment for such a young writer. It was the first book I ever read by her. I remember getting a copy of it from a bookshop at Emerald Isle beach in my native state of North Carolina. The children's book, written for people of all ages, deals with the problem of evil, time travel, tesseract, and the triumph of Christ's love over hate and evil. After reading the other books in the series, I wanted to read her non-fiction.

Madeleine L' Engle's *Walking On Water Reflections On Faith and Art* is the best book I have ever read about the importance of imagination, reason and its limits, the healing power of art, and how faith, daily life, and art all correlate, and the discipline it takes to be an artist and cultivate your craft. L' Engle's book also helped smash to bits a false dichotomy I had in my paradigm about what is sacred and what is secular art. For years I struggled with this either/or, and thought Southern Gospel music and Hymns were sacred, whereas classic rock, country, folk, and Celtic music was secular and worldly. This troubled my mind greatly and caused a great deal of confusion. How freeing it was when this wonderful book came my way and conveyed to me that this ignorant approach to art is erroneous, and that art is something universal that brings together people of many different worldviews and cultural backgrounds. I read this book at the time in my life just when I needed too!

I remember underlining many passages, memorizing quotes, and finding it be a very challenging, encouraging, and fascinating read. At that time I read it, I was struggling to find my voice as a writer, but it was a start, and this book was one that really helped me find my voice, as well as others by C. S. Lewis, George MacDonald, Robert Frost, John Steinbeck, and Jane Austen.

Re-reading it again for the second time reminded me of why I love writing, that good writing is very, very, hard work, and that a writer must write every day, whether it is a thousand words, or one little paragraph written after a very tiring day of work when you just want to crawl in bed and call it a night.

Some of my favorite moments in the book is when L'Engle quotes and references George MacDonald, the struggle and joy she experienced when her iconic book *A Wrinkle In Time* was published, her important belief in the fact that there is no sacred or secular either/or, and that whatever the artist worldview, their belief will come out in their work, and the many other references to great writers, composers, painters, and other artists that she herself found to be of great help as she was pursuing her vocation.

L'Engle gives a very valid point about not comparing your own unique gift and voice to the great artists that have come before, but to build off of them, find your own voice, perfect your craft, and to surrender to the work itself. When working on different creative projects, the transcendent experiences I have had, has filled me with wonder and great joy.

I once met a lady who knew Madeleine L'Engle, and she spoke very highly of her. That was an amazing moment, and I am glad that she wrote the books she did.

John Steinbeck

At a local coffee shop called *the Dripolator* in downtown Black Mountain, North Carolina, there is a local regular who I call "Steinbeck" when I always see him. I started calling him that after he recommended Steinbeck's *Cannery Row* and *Sweet Thursday* - which is the superior of the two in his opinion. The gritty humble and prolific writer from the Salinas valley in California got me very excited about an epic trip to Ireland, Scotland, and England that I took in 2021 when I read his book *Travels with Charley in Search of America.*

Reading that book about Steinbeck traveling all over the States with his French poodle gave me wanderlust, and caused me to be filled with panic about my trip not working out because of the coronavirus pandemic, and also great joy if it did work out, because I had not seen my dear friends in the British Isles in three years, and I had never been to bonny Scotland or Ireland. After that life changing trip, when I got back home to the mountains of North Carolina, I didn't get a dog, or go on an epic road trip like Steinbeck did which he recorded in his fascinating, funny, disturbing, and moving travel memoir, but looking back in retrospect, that book gave me hope that the much yearned for trip would work, and I am so thankful that it did.

Jon Foreman

Autumn, to me, is the most glorious season. I love the cool, crisp, invigorating air, the changing of the leaves to striking yellow, red, orange, and gold, Halloween, harvest time, apple cider, long walks, hearing the leaves crunching under my feet, and it is the best time to re-read Robert Frost's poem *October,* John Keats' *To Autumn,* and Ray Bradbury's book *The October Country.* A music album that evokes this glorious of all seasons, is the musician Jon Foreman's *Fall ep.* The melancholy of *Southbound Train* makes me feel like I am taking a long train ride in the rain staring out the window in a very pensive mode, and *The Cure For Pain,* is an honest prayer about doubt and faith.

Foreman is a very prolific musician, and it was his music years ago that sowed the seed for me to find a passion for writing, literature, and art. One of the best experiences of my life was giving him a copy of my book *Surprised By Agape,* published by Grant Hudson of Clarendon House Publications, on his birthday. I got to talk with him for a bit, and express my debt of gratitude for the profound impact his music has had on my faith and understanding of art. He expressed great gratitude, gave me a hug, and thanked me. I have seen him play numerous times, and I appreciate how he connects with the audience, the passion with which he puts into his music, his honesty about his doubts, and his faith, and his love for his wife, kids, and friends. Jon Foreman is like a modern-day Bob Dylan or Rich Mullins. His *Fall, Winter, Summer, Spring,* and *The Wonderlands* albums are all amazing, but my favorite by him, is his most recent one called *Departures. Jesus I have My Doubts, Thanks Be to God, Red & Gold, Side by Side,* and all the other songs are good, but my favorite is *The Ocean Beyond The Sea.* It evokes sehnsucht joy, and I know Jon Foreman must have had a glimpse of Tír na nÓg to be able to write that song. Thanks for doing what you do Jon Foreman.

Ray Bradbury

When you look up at the vast expanse of the starry night sky and think about how vast the cosmos is, it is quite humbling, and all kinds of thoughts and questions can come to your mind. Are there are other types of beings in the universe? If so, are they hostile to us, or are they like us human beings? What would their religion, spirituality, art, and culture be like? These kinds of questions inspired the great science fiction and fantasy writer Ray Bradbury to write his fascinating book *The Martian Chronicles,* and his love for books, libraries, and art, inspired him to write *Fahrenheit 451.* Of the two, the latter is my favorite. The story is quite a sobering dystopian tale about technology becoming a god, virtual reality becoming objective reality, books being banned and burned, and the utter extinguishing of free thought and philosophical inquiry.

Bradbury found much of the modern world quite frustrating because of how reliant people are on technology for many things. Even if you have a good balance with technology, it can feel quite strange that we are so reliant on it, and that there are so many things at our fingertips that we can look up, which is mind-blowing. Bradbury also found much of the modern world scary because he feared less, and less people would take the time to read books. To him books were essential. Indeed, they are sacramental objects. Books can evoke a certain mood, a certain emotion, can make you cry, laugh, and can move you so profoundly that they change your life. This has happened to me numerous times, and it also did to Bradbury, which is evident in his prolific career. I am very thankful the eccentric writer from Illinois spent his life emphasizing the importance of reading, the importance of books, and art in daily life.

Wendell Berry

The first time I ever became aware of the poet and farmer Wendell Berry, was when I read his poem *The Peace of Wild Things*. The journalist and writer Phillip Yancey quoted it in his book called *Prayer*. I sat inside a Starbucks and re-read that poem numerous times and wanted to become more acquainted with his writings, so I did just that. That poem has often come to my mind while hiking at favorite haunts in the mountains of North Carolina where I live, and indeed, the poem conveys that amazing truth of finding peace and rejuvenation while being out in nature. For different people, that is hiking the Camino, the Appalachian Trail, walking down a beach during a sunrise or sunset, surfing, skiing, camping, backpacking, or simply going on a favorite walk in a wood, a park, or neighborhood.

Wendell Berry conveys in his writings, and the way he lives his life, the importance of being a steward of the earth and doing good in your community. He is very admired and respected by many people who are finding sustainable farming to be a vocation, as well environmentalists, foresters, professors, writers, poets, mechanics, doctors, gardeners, artists, and people of many different vocations. He critiques the view that Nature is something a human being owns and that can be sold for money and manipulated to one's will, at whatever cost. This way of viewing nature is evidence of the dark side of human nature- the work of Mordor to reference Tolkien. In the one novel, essays, and other poetry I have read by Wendell Berry, he has made me take self-sufficiency more seriously, and challenges me to plant a tree, a garden, to be useful to my community in my writings, and find different ways to serve. These are things that I am working on, and it has helped me to take more seriously the commandment to live out the agape love of Christ.

Scotland

Robert Louis Stevenson

I remember first learning about the book *Treasure Island* from an entertaining PBS show called *Wishbone* which involved a dog impersonating famous characters from literature. The show did a great job with introducing classic books to kids all over the world in a modern day context - the idea about the dog was very clever, because what human being doesn't like a loyal and amusing dog?

It would be years later when I first read the iconic book written by the Scotsman Robert Louis Stevenson. *Treasure Island* was a very fun read, and it popularized pirates in modern pop culture - a good example of this is *The Pirates of the Caribbean* film series starring the brilliant iconic Johnny Depp as Captain Jack Sparrow. If you enjoy stories about travel on the high seas, mythology, danger, peril, love, courage, and epic adventure, then this book, and the film series is for you. My friend Andrew rebuked me for not watching all of the *Pirates of the Caribbean Films,* and so I remedied that very quickly, and was glad that I did.

As good as *Treasure Island* is, I found myself more so enjoying *The Strange Case of Dr. Jekyll and Mr. Hyde.* The book is very brilliant in how it captures human duality of darkness and light within every individual and is an important reminder of how powerful the choices that we make are.

What I aim for each day that I live is to surrender to the 'Hyde' aspect of myself and embrace the 'Jekyll' part that is truly Justin Wiggins, seeking goodness, beauty, truth, joy, and love over lust, darkness, and worship of mammon and self.

It is fascinating to me that Stevenson ended up living among the Samoan people in his last years, and he became highly revered by them. It was quite a long way from his homeland of Scotland. I appreciate Stevenson's sense of adventure, his love for travel, culture, literature, and some of his prayers I have read compiled in a wonderful book compiled by his wife called Prayers. I look forward to reading more Stevenson!

George MacDonald

Scotland is a fascinating and beautiful country that has given the world some of the greatest poets, musicians, and artists, and writers. One of those great writers from the Isle of Alba is the Scottish writer, poet, and mythmaker George MacDonald. MacDonald was descended from a clan that was almost completely slaughtered at the massacre at Glencoe. The place is said to be haunted, and it is a miracle that MacDonald himself came into existence. MacDonald is sadly not as widely read as C. S. Lewis would have liked him to be, which is one reason why Lewis compiled his *George MacDonald An Anthology* in 1946.

The first time I came across the book, I was browsing around in a Barnes and Noble and when I read these words, tears came to my eyes:

"That man is perfect in faith who can come to God in the utter dearth of his feelings and desires, without a glow or an aspiration, with the weight of low thoughts, failures, neglects, and wandering forgetfulness, and say to Him, 'Thou art my refuge.'" (George MacDonald An Anthology, Lewis.) (5)

A line like that comes from a human being who has a profound understanding, by experience and not the intellect alone, that we are all loved by a good and loving Creator. For MacDonald to come to this kind of hopeful view in his life, took a great deal of unlearning a fierce hyper-Calvinism which was deeply ingrained in the Scottish culture he grew up in.

Many readers have found solace in MacDonald's theology because they themselves have been deeply wounded by some negative experience with organized religion which involved brainwashing. The God George MacDonald came to believe in was greater than a vindictive Jove or Zeus-like deity that cared only for having its wrath appeased or its beloved glory on display. The God he believed in came for the rescue of all of humanity in the first century through Jesus of Nazareth's Incarnation, Death, and Resurrection — agape love on display which is greater than sin, death, and the powers of hell. What mortal can comprehend that great depth of everlasting love?

Here in 2021, many more people are discovering the writings of MacDonald through word of mouth, articles, blogs online, through Inklings' conferences, scholarly papers and books inspired by his theology and literary legacy, and through my Scottish friend David Jack's translations of MacDonald's novels from the Doric into English. David is a very good friend, and has done an amazing job with these new translations through the *worksofmacdonald.com website.*

My most cherished book by MacDonald is a Penguin

edition book of his fairy tales that I got from Waterstones in Oxford, England when I was with David Jack. That book brings back a very special memory.

In his life, George MacDonald went through much failure pursuing a career as a preacher, struggled with poverty, suffered quite a lot, but yet was a great Scotsman of faith, a good husband, father, a prolific writer, friends with Mark Twain, Alfred Lord Tennyson, John Ruskin, and left behind quite an amazing literary legacy. I understand more and more why C. S. Lewis praised his writings so much, and I am very glad that many people today are discovering the rich works of George MacDonald. The Scotsman should be as well-known as Sir Walter Scott, Robert Burns, J. M. Barrie, and Robert Louis Stevenson!

One of the most baffling things I ever experienced was once when I met these wonderful people at a favorite local coffee shop, heard their Scottish accents, and we struck up a good conversation about Scotland and different writers. "Have you ever heard of George MacDonald?" I asked with great excitement. They shook their heads with a blank stare and responded with, "No, we haven't." I gladly recommended MacDonald to them. The rest of the conversation was quite pleasant, but I was very perplexed that these kind and charming people from Scotland had never heard of one of the greatest writers that came out of

Scotland — it would be like if I had lived in Russia and never heard of Leo Tolstoy or Fyodor Dostoevsky.

The first book that I ever read by George MacDonald was *The Princess and The Goblin*. The particular edition I read was a worn Penguin children's classic that was less than five dollars. As I was reading through it, I imagined George MacDonald writing it with a smile on his face, and then telling this enchanting and captivating tale to his children and wife as they gathered around the fireplace to listen to this story which would eventually become a classic. In the story, Irene's great grandmother is, to some degree, like Aslan in Lewis's Narnia series — she is mysterious, strong, wise, ancient, and wild but also good.

After I finished the story, I found myself loving Christ more, and became a devoted admirer of MacDonald — I wanted to read everything that the Scotsman wrote, and biographies on him, so I could understand why he was so revered by many writers, though he is still not as well known today as he should be, which is quite baffling. Many young people in my generation have suffered the appalling reality of being abandoned by a father or mother. This great wound causes difficult and complex issues with depression, trauma, anxiety, and this constant fear of being abandoned even by people who are always there for you.

Although George MacDonald sadly lost his mother at a

very young age, he was fortunate to have a loving father who was truly there for him. One of the most important aspects of MacDonald's writings is his description of agape love — Cosmo's bond with his father from *Castle Warlock,* Robert being reunited with his father who was a former addict in *Robert Falconer,* and the fairy godmother figure in his fairy tales. I praise Christ for the great Scotsman.

Sir Walter Scott

How fitting it was to pick a copy of Sir Walter Scott's *Rob Roy* at a Waterstones in Dundee, Scotland when I was with my Scottish friend David Jack. Other than David's great enthusiasm for the great Scottish writer, and references to his life and writings in essays and letters by writers I admire, I didn't know much about him, nor, sadly, had I read anything by him save some of his poems like *The Lady of the Lake, The Lake Minstrel,* and *The Lord of the Isles.* These were poems written by a Scotsman that had a great love for myth and classical literature, and who defined the historical fiction genre with his Waverly novels. His novels are filled with fascinating insights into the Jacobite uprisings, Scottish Highland culture, peril, courage, and great love stories. Robert Louis Stevenson said of Scott's Rob Roy,

"When I think of Rob Roy, I am impatient with all other novels.; they seem to but shadows and impostors; they cannot satisfy the appetite which this awakened." (6)

That is high praise indeed coming from one Scottish writer to another.

The popular historical fiction genre today owes it origin to Scott's Waverly novels. In the context of modern-day culture, a good example of this is Diana

Gabaldon's Outlander series. Some readers don't like it of course, but the Amazon Prime series, as well as the books, have become part of 21st century consciousness-people have become quite zealous about it, just as many did when J.R.R. Tolkien's *The Lord of the Rings* first came out, as well as J.K. Rowling's *Harry Potter* series.

One friend of mine who was not really interested in history, read the Outlander series, and she became absolutely obsessed with the 17th century. When I was in Scotland enjoying some Haggis, the company of my Scottish friends, and a pint of Guinness, this very nice Scottish lady who was our server grinned when she saw my copy of the first book I got in Perth, Scotland. We owe it to Sir Walter Scott for defining the historical fiction genre of literature, and he is a great writer from the Isle of Alba that I am thankful for.

It is good to enjoy a wee dram of McClelland's or Glenfiddich and immerse yourself in the exciting works of Sir Walter Scott. If you aren't Scottish, his writing will make you wish that you were, as well as George MacDonald's.

Poems

Ode to Myth

Stories told around bonfires,
sacred groves, stone circles, mead halls,
and under the stars
That help us understand why we are here and
who we are,
Are retold in many different and unique ways,
In a universal language, through poetry, prose,
film, painting, and dance,
Many important transcendent truths they
convey.

Ode to Books

Some of my best hours,

Have been spent immersed in a paperback or hardback book,

Language has a great power,

Of bringing one tears of sorrow, empathy, laughter, and joy,

Whether by a fireside, in a pub, a coffee shop,

Or in an Autumn, Winter, Spring, or Summer wood.

Mystical Mountains

During Autumn, Winter, Summer, and

Spring,

These primitive majestic mountains

To my soul, they bring

Transcendent joy, artistic inspiration

And an awareness that I am not alone,

In the cosmos

Despite my doubt

The Great Artist is making all things new

Through work, rest, art, comedy, compassion, love,

And mystical mountain views.

Ode to Oxford & North Carolina

Flying on a plane for the first time,

Bound for Oxford, England, only to find,

A joy I had never experienced before,

Like the Pevensie children walking into the magic of

Narnia

through the wardrobe door,

In awe browsing and reading at The Bodleian and

Blackwell's,

Purchasing books by admired writers who loved The

Greatest

Teller of True Tales,

Walking Addison's walk, writing, reading, and

enjoying rich

conversation at The Eagle and Child,

The never experienced joy is bittersweet, mystical, and

wild,

Flying on a plane for the second time,

To North Carolina, only to find,

The primitive majestic mountains — my shire, my

home — as

well as Oxford — a prayer of gratitude I pray

An ode to Oxford and North Carolina — another way I

have

been Surprised by Agape!

Autumn

Sing little feathered one,

Thy rapturous song of Autumn's reign;

Ere long her leaves shall fall and be gone As old man

winter makes his frigid way.

But for now I sing with you little feathered one,

Every note of Autumn's beauty and mirth; Ere long,
you shall be gone, Leaving the sweetest song that
maketh my heart leap up

Birthday in Dublin

For many years, I yearned to see,

The birthplace of C. S. Lewis, John O'Donohue, and Seamus Heaney,

And by grace, there I was in the year 2021,

Marveling at the beauty of the Irish sea

On my birthday I walked the hallowed streets of Dublin,

With great excitement and joy,

Enjoyed good coffee, purchased books from Hodges Figgis,

Enjoy good pints of Guinness at the factory,

And raised a toast to Heaney, Yeats, O'Donohue, Lewis, and Joyce.

Stories

The Writer

That week in March memories of Oxford, England often came back to the writers' mind from three years ago. He remembered what it was like first visiting the pub his favorite writer would go to join his friends at for a pint, good laughs, and rich conversation. He remembered visiting his favorite writers' home, The Kilns, the cold, rain, snow, and beauty of the English countryside, the many books purchased, seeing old friends, making new friends, numerous pints, cups of coffee, meeting locals, the stunning architecture, and old colleges, feeding a very hungry duck, and writing some of his first book there. Reliving these experiences made him even more thankful to be alive during the coronavirus pandemic that his human tribe had going through for the past year. Many of his favorite writers, thinkers, musicians, and artists had lived through war, disease, political turmoil, and famine, and in their own small way, sought to create honest art that would express universal questions and doubts, and also remind people of joy, hope, make them laugh, and remind them of the gift of love, music, literature, and life.

The writer sought to do that in his own book - if he could write something honest and hopeful that people of different worldviews could resonate with, and that would be something encouraging and inspiring, it would be something worth doing even if it didn't pay much. The utilitarian view of art in the instant gratification culture in which he lived was not within his paradigm. He learned early on that he must write because he loved it and not to do it to just try and make money. Many writers had normal day jobs, and also struggled, just like he did. He doubted himself quite often, found it hard not to compare himself to others who seemed to be living the ideal life, often felt quite stuck, was his own worst critic, struggled with past trauma, anxiety, and depression, and sometimes doubted what he professed, though paradoxically his faith was strengthened in this way.

He would do certain rituals such as go for walk, a hike, meditate, pray, read a favorite book, poem, watch a film, or get coffee, tea, a meal, or a pint with a friend. These rituals helped him get out of his head, combat depression, remind him of what he had accomplished, how much he had to be thankful for, and the gift of each breath. The artistic community of people in his life also inspired and encouraged him to keep writing, dreaming, working hard, relaxing, laughing, growing, and exude goodness and beauty. He smiled as he enjoyed a good cup of coffee after a chaotic busy day of work and looked out on the primitive, beautiful, and majestic mountains. The writer had great joy in the present chapter of his life and looked forward to the future with great fascination. He was glad to be a writer.

The Bard & The Faerie Queen

Once upon a time there lived an orphan who yearned to be a bard. This orphan's name was Blagan, and he would feel indescribable joy when he heard the different bards that came to his poor village to sing songs of humor, loss, joy, and love. While listening to the bards he would feel less alone and have a glimpse of what his life could possibly be like. Perhaps he would eventually find someone he could appreciate and love, find decent paying work that would bring joy to people, and like his parents, be enough of a warrior to protect his clan from evil beings. These thoughts gave him great hope, even though his village had been attacked recently by fearsome creatures of the night that drank the blood of their victims, and he suffered a terrible loss. Blagan's beloved Father and Mother had been killed in the recent attack, and the time of peace in the village had ended. Blagan's father Angus and Mother Isobel were blacksmith's, warriors, farmers, musicians, and vampire slayers. They had killed who they thought was the leader of the coven, but it turned out to be only the mate of the leader, and when the leader Dracula found his mate Lilith impaled on a stake and nothing but ash, he vowed revenge on the slayers and their son, and revenge gripped him like a madness.

One Midsummer night when the villagers were preparing to protect themselves from another anticipated attack, Bard was sitting in a small cottage, feeling frightened for his life while keeping watch over the young bard that had sung in the village that day , when all of a sudden, the cheerful fire went out, and he heard the horrifying growling sounds of the vampires, the screams of the villagers, and in an instant found himself powerless, and being gripped by the throat of the most feared evil being and father of all the undead.

"I must have my revenge and your blood young mortal, for you are a greater threat to me and my kind more than you know"

said Dracula in his seductive and malicious voice that made Blagan tremble in his skin. The dark prince broke Blagan's sword in two and was about to sink his fangs into his neck, when all of a sudden, the bard began to sing a hymn to the Mother Goddess, which had not been sung in that land for thousands of years. The bard continued to sing, and Blagan began to sing to the hymn in unison. Dracula had heard this song before time began, but this time, it was his last, for he and all his brood of hell disintegrated and were defeated. Blagan stared in awe as the hood of the bard was pulled back, and he saw The Faerie Queen herself, whose beauty and ethereal presence made him fall to his knees, while she made him a bard. And that is the story of how Humankind and the Fae became one.

The Barista & The Bookseller

Lucy paused from her reading, took a sip of her delicious cappuccino, and stared out the window of the local coffee shop that she liked to frequent. The passage she read from Madeleine L'Engle's *Walking On Water Reflections On Faith & Art* about how healing it is for an artist to write something honest and hopeful for people of all worldviews, brought many vivid memories to her mind of sorrow and joy-it made her miss her dear friend Maeve. Maeve had sadly recently died unexpectedly, and it was a heavy blow from which she would never fully recover from in this life-indeed, who does? Yet, Lucy found herself immensely thankful for the impact Maeve had on her life, understanding of art, and her worldview. She deeply cherished the memories they made together in Ireland.

Lucy first met Maeve when she was on a study abroad trip for a literature course in Dublin, Ireland. Lucy didn't have many friends yet in Dublin, and she was excited about all the rich experiences yet to happen and about cultivating a community. Lucy was the type of person that could find a common bond with anyone. One night she was at a local pub where a poetry and music open mic night was happening, and as she was sitting reading over her poem that she was going to share, the girl sitting next to her was talking and laughing with a good-looking Irishman with dark hair and blue eyes. When Lucy noticed a copy of John O' Donohue's *Anam Cara* and *100 Poems* by Seamus Heaney beside the lass and lad enjoying good banter and conversation, she decided to do what she usually did in such situations and say hello. Maeve and her brother Colin instantly became friends with her. They talked with great excitement about the beauty of the mountains of North Carolina, the beauty of Ireland, music, books, writers, culture, art, food, and much from life experience. That night Lucy made two good friends for life as the talk became much richer, and the numerous pints and food were enjoyed after the open mic night, and it was also the night Colin and Lucy became immensely fascinated by each other.

During Lucy's time in Ireland, Maeve and Colin showed her all their favorite haunts, coffeeshops, pubs, and the true definition of Irish hospitality. When it was time for Lucy to go back to America after her study abroad was over, she reluctantly said goodbye to Maeve and Colin, especially to Colin since they were engaged to be married that year. Lucy still remembered seeing them both as she was getting ready to board her plane sadly.

Lucy received the news of Maeve being diagnosed with cancer a week after she had been back in the states. It was hard for her to concentrate on her teaching and barista jobs, and the locals started to notice that she was not her usual jovial self. One bitter winter day Lucy got an emergency call from Colin about the direness of the situation after things had looked somewhat hopeful for Maeve, and that night Lucy packed her bags and was on a plane to Ireland. It broke her heart to see her strong and resilient friend Maeve go through such horrific suffering. Maeve still managed to make her laugh with her witty jokes and move her deeply when she would read one of her poems to her. One cold January day, Maeve looked into Lucy's face with such a defiant sense of hope, and said to her in her sweet Irish voice, "There is one thing I request before I leave this life for good. I want to see you and my brother Colin get married. I have a Claddagh ring given to me by my Grandmother Hilda, and I want you to have it. So, well, propose to my brother Colin, and may your wild wedding night make all the gods and lovers jealous!" Lucy laughed and cried tears of sorrow and joy as she took the Claddagh ring gently from Maeve and held her hand. "You damn right I will! By God and the Gods, I will be honored to marry your brother Colin in your presence under an Irish sky."

And it was that very week Lucy proposed to Colin in front of Maeve and all the family. They were married under an Irish sky just as Maeve wanted, and the wedding was the most beautiful thing she had ever experienced in her life. She expressed great joy to her brother and Lucy, and the lovers and gods were certainly jealous of their wedding night. Weeks later Maeve passed away, with Lucy and Colin by her side, and in her honor, they decided to open up a bookshop that was also a coffee shop called *The Bookseller & The Barista* in Dublin. It was always one of Maeve's dreams to open her own bookshop, and her brother and Lucy fulfilled that dream. They felt like Maeve was there in spirit, and it became quite a popular place for many of the locals, and people traveling to Ireland from around the world. Lucy found great solace and joy in re-reading Madeleine L'Engle's *Walking On Water Reflections On Faith & Art*. It was Maeve's favorite book, and she left her signed copy as a gift to Lucy as a wedding gift.

Healing Celtic Song

Jack was going through a difficult season of grief and managing as best as he could. Boston would never be the same place again. Since his youth, his brother Finn was always there - like Frodo and Sam. The Irish neighborhood they grew up in was quite poor, but a very close community where everyone knew everybody, and Jack desperately wanted to be loved and always felt like the black sheep of the tribe. Finn always made him feel like he belonged and showed him his full potential, especially with his pursuit of music. Jack would watch many of the other kids in the neighborhood play violin, fiddle, guitar, banjo, bass, and the flute without much effort, and always envied how good they were. One fine summer day his brother Finn saw him crying in his room and comforted him by letting him play his beloved fiddle. Finn taught him at his own pace, and Jack got very good, and found great joy in playing his brother's fiddle. Music became a passion that became a vocation.

Trying to cope with the loss of his musician brother Finn who lost his battle with cancer, hurt like hell, and at times seemed unbearable. It was hard for him to come to grips with him being gone. Finn was there for him during his darkest times, and he felt utterly alone, and didn't know how to deal with the pain. Suicide was out of the picture, since he had been through all that hell in his past, and sought the long road to recovery, with Finn by his side believing in him.

When everything had almost been taken from Jack during that dark night of the soul he went through in the past, it was the love of his brother Finn, and their love for music which helped him cope and find shalom in the chaos of life.

One day after an appointment with his counselor, Jack got home and decided to be brave instead of cutting off the lights and going to sleep. For months he had been cutting people off, isolating himself, not joining his friends at the local *October Leaves* coffeeshop he would get together to talk with about books, music, and art, but this evening, courage welled up within him, and he became more aware of the brevity of life as he got his brothers fiddle out and started to play, and he was damn glad he did.

The next day he showed up at work to the shock of his boss Angus, and with great zeal and enthusiasm talked with many customers about his love for music and different instruments. The regulars that came in were glad to see him. That particular Autumn Day, a new face walked in the guitar shop. Jack noticed her dark raven hair, luminous blue eyes, and was delighted to hear her Irish accent. After an enthusiastic talk about music, art, and Irish culture with Brigid McArthur, she invited Jack to one of her shows at *October Leaves,* and he gladly accepted.

Jack walked into *October Leaves* on a cool crisp Autumn evening with a great sense of Finn being there with him after a great day of work. He smiled and tears came to his eyes as he remembered the last conversation they had together. He missed his brother so much and wished that he was there, but he knew he was there in spirit. At first, he couldn't bear to visit the places they would frequent, had to take some time off work, and could hardly get out of bed, but that was many months ago, and now he was in a much better state of being. Jack was glad to be at October *Leaves* for a good chat, coffee, and to hear his recently made friend Brigid McArthur play some Celtic music.

Jack was deeply moved as he listened to Brigid play traditional Irish songs, and shared some of her own songs about grief, loss, doubt, pub culture, joy, love, the gift of life, and the healing power of art. The last song she played was by far Jack's favorite. As she sang the words, he became one with the melody, and wept as she told her story through song of what it was like being homeless, and how through much pain and trauma, she persevered by the virtue of hope and found a passion that became a vocation. After she played and the crowd's applause, Brigid had a good chat with Jack over coffee. As she spoke, he looked into her blue eyes and found himself immensely fascinated by her. About six months later her album came out, Jack finished a novel dedicated to his brother which was published, and they were married in Ireland.

Tír na nÓg

It was a very cold beautiful January day in the mountains of North Carolina, and Fiona was thinking of her Nana Lydia McArthur who had passed away recently - the Matriarch of the family lived a good full and long life. Her Nana Lydia McArthur emigrated from Dublin, Ireland with her husband Patrick to America, taught elementary school for many years, and was well known in Black Mountain for helping the poor, needy, and broken, as well as for her wit, humor, and bardic gift of storytelling.

As Fiona paused from reading C. S. Lewis's *The Magician's Nephew*, she smelled the pleasant aroma of her hot chocolate, and stared into the dancing flames of the fire, and remembered her Irish grandmother telling her stories about the Tuatha dé Danann and Tír na nÓg - the isle of the eternal youth, her love for Lewis's Narnia books, and great Irish poets like William Butler Yeats, Seamus Heaney, and the ancient Celtic myths. Her Nana's voice came vividly to her mind, as she remembered being spellbound while listening and marveling at the great storyteller her Nana was. Tears of joyful remembrance trickled slowly down her cheeks. From her Nana, she got her red hair, her bright green eyes, wit, intelligence, sense of intuition, belief in the goodness and agape love of The Great Artist, and great courage, which would soon be tested.

The next few weeks while Fiona was on Winter break from teaching literature at the local community college, she started to feel quite weak, have frequent nose bleeds when out in public to her utter embarrassment at her favorite coffee shops and bookstores, felt very nauseated and started to lose weight. This all greatly alarmed Fiona, because her Mother, Colleen, had lost her battle with cancer, when she was only ten years old, and was raised by her Nana and Grandfather Patrick. The symptoms were undeniable, and so Fiona went to her family doctor to find out what she truly knew was the issue. To her utter horror she was diagnosed with cancer.

The road to recovery seemed to Fiona, very dark and grim. She lost her hair, went to chemo, and eventually became very tired of hospitals, and missed her colleagues and students, and her great courage began to dwindle in the face of death. She still wanted to travel to Ireland, Scotland, Wales, and Cornwall, and find someone she could cook with, joke around with, read and drink with, and that would make her feel loved and appreciated.

Conor O' Reilly, the owner of the local coffee shop in Black Mountain, had been told of Fiona's current depressing state by her Grandfather, who was a regular there. Conor was absolutely horrified upon hearing the news. Fiona was well loved and appreciated by many in the community and was such a radiant person of hope and joy that everyone found contagious. Conor, and many around the community, began raising funds to help cover Fiona's hospital bills, and other than her Grandfather Patrick,

Conor became the one to visit her regularly. He brought her books, chocolates, her favorite coffee, and tea, sang to her, made her laugh, read with her, and tried to ease her suffering. This was not easy for Conor, because he had lost his sister to cancer the previous year, and she had her whole life ahead of her. He hated cancer, and it was breaking his heart to see his friend Fiona go through so much suffering.

Some days she was a broken mess, and other days, she was in good spirits. One evening after Conor got home after a long day of work and visitng with Fiona, he picked up his guitar and pen, and started writing a song to help combat his own grief and confusion, to remind himself of goodness and beauty. That evening Fiona found herself very depressed, and all kinds of imaginative scenarios were going through her mind - she was facing a wretched illness not knowing if she would make it or not.

She glanced over at the books Conor brought her, and one of the books was a first edition of *The Magician's Nephew* by C.S. Lewis. She picked it up, and as she began to read, precious memories of her Nana came back to her mind telling her of Tír na nÓg, as well as precious moments of the past year-she was very thankful for her community. Before she went to sleep, she said a prayer of gratitude, just simply thankful for all the beauty in her life.

Over the next year, the friendship between Fiona and Conor started to turn into romantic love, and though it was very risky for them both, they both came to a place of surrender, and gladly chose each other. To everyone's utter joy in the Black Mountain community, Fiona began to get better. Her red hair grew back, she beat the cancer and felt strong again, went back to teaching, and that summer, went on an epic adventure to Ireland, Wales, Cornwall, England, and Scotland, and it was in Ireland where Fiona and Conor had a handfasting ceremony of marriage. It was the best day of their lives, and one they looked back on with joy in the years to come.

Afterword

During a very bitter Winter, years ago, I felt like it was a curse to be a conscious human being on the planet, and that faith, or anything divine (whatever it might be) was a delusion, so I decided to give up. I did not desire that, but the pain was so damn unbearable that I couldn't bear it any longer. Yet, as Providence would have it, I survived suicide, and years later, wonder of wonders, I found myself stable, able to hold down a job, surrounded by an artistic community, immensely thankful for my family and friends, the author of four books, and filled with an epic sense of joy to be alive-the same poignant joy Frodo and Sam felt when returning to The Shire after the evil ring was destroyed, or the same way Reepicheep felt when he found himself finally in Aslan's country that he had always longed for since a Dryad sang a prophetic song over him when he was a wee mouse.

My trip to Ireland, Scotland, and England, was a great reminder to me of how far I have come, and that, despite my doubts, The Great Artist is making all things new. I got a glimpse of Tír na nÓg when I was in bonny Scotland, Ireland, and England, just like my favorite writer, C. S. Lewis did, many times in his life.

Works Cited

1) James, Joyce. *Dubliners.* Penguin Books. USA, 1993.

2) Wilde, Oscar. *The Selfish Giant.* https://www.wilde-online.info/the-selfish-giant-page3.html

3) Keats, John. The Complete Poems of John Keats. Modern Library Edition. New York, 1994.

4) Shakespeare, William. *Twelfth Night* http://shakespeare.mit.edu/twelfth_night/full.html

5) Lewis, C. S. *George MacDonald: An Anthology.* William Collins, Great Britain 2016.

6) Scott, Sir Walter. *Rob Roby.* Penguin Books. Great Britain, 1995.

About the Author

Justin Wiggins is a local author that works and lives in the primitive, majestic, beautiful mountains of North Carolina. He graduated with his Bachelor's in English Literature from Montreat College with a focus on C. S. Lewis studies in May of 2018. His first book was Surprised by Agape, published by Grant Hudson of Clarendon House Publications, his second book, Surprised By Myth, he co-wrote with Grant Hudson, was published in Autumn of 2021, and his third book, Marty & Irene, was published in November of 2021 by Steve Cawte of Impspired. He has also had poems, and other short pieces published by Clarendon House Publications, the C. S. Lewis Sehnshuct Journal, and by Sweety Cat Press. Justin has a great zeal for life, work, community, writing, literature, art, pubs, bookstores, and coffee shops. His fourth book, Tír na nÓg, was published in 2022 by Steve Cawte of Impspired.

www.ingramcontent.com/pod-product-compliance
Lightning Source LLC
Chambersburg PA
CBHW061004050726
47592CB00003B/1339

* 9 7 8 1 9 1 4 1 3 0 5 4 0 *